Management and Cost Accounting

Fourth Edition

Alnoor Bhimani
Charles T. Horngren
Srikant M. Datar
George Foster

 Blac

Supplement

PROFESSIONAL EXAM QUESTIONS FROM

PAST *ACCA*, *CIMA*, AND *ICAI* PAPERS

with selected answers

Compiled by
Tianjing Dai

 **FT** Prentice Hall
FINANCIAL TIMES

An imprint of Pearson Education
Harlow, England • London • New York • Boston • San Francisco • Toronto
Sydney • Tokyo • Singapore • Hong Kong • Seoul • Taipei • New Delhi
Cape Town • Madrid • Mexico City • Amsterdam • Munich • Paris • Milan

Pearson Education Limited
Edinburgh Gate
Harlow
Essex CM20 2JE
England

and Associated Companies throughout the world

Visit us on the World Wide Web at:
www.pearsoned.co.uk

First published 2002
Fourth edition published 2008

ISBN: 978-0-273-71153-7

10 9 8 7 6 5

10 09

6829285
658.1511 DAI
13.5-10 PA
~~SHORT~~ STD.

Printed in the United Kingdom by Henry Ling Limited, at the Dorset Press, Dorchester, DT1 1HD

Introduction

This booklet contains over 30 questions from past ACCA, CIMA and ICAI papers, plus suggested answers to selected questions.

Answers to some of the questions are included in this booklet, allowing students to test their understanding of key topics and prepare for exams.

The answers to the remaining questions are available on the password-protected lecturer side of the companion website that supports this book at:

www.pearsoned.co.uk/bhimani

This allows tutors to set selected questions for assignments and seminar use.

Acknowledgements

Our thanks to Tianjing Dai for selecting the questions and sourcing the answers.

We are grateful to the following for permission to reproduce examination questions: Association of Chartered Certified Accountants (ACCA); Institute of Chartered Accountants in Ireland (ICAI); and Chartered Institute of Management Accountants (CIMA). The copyright of the questions belongs to ACCA, ICAI or CIMA and permission to reproduce these questions should be directed to the appropriate organisation. The examination boards are not responsible for the suggested answers to questions. The suggested answers have been provided by the author.

Supporting resources
Visit **www.pearsoned.co.uk/bhimani** to find valuable online resources

Companion Website for students
- Self-assessment questions with Grade Tracker function to test your learning and monitor your progress
- Learning objectives for each chapter
- A mix of multiple choice, fill-in-the-blank and true/false questions to help test your learning
- Annotated links to relevant sites on the web
- An online glossary to explain key terms

For instructors
- Complete, downloadable Instructor's Manual with teaching ideas and solutions to professional questions from the main text
- PowerPoint slides that can be downloaded and used for presentations
- Suggested solutions to all case study material
- Solutions to additional questions and spreadsheet problems
- Testbank of question material

Also: The Companion Website with Grade Tracker provides the following features:

- Search tool to help locate specific items of content
- E-mail results and profile tools to send results of quizzes to instructors
- Online help and support to assist with website usage and troubleshooting

For more information please contact your local Pearson Education sales representative
or visit **www.pearsoned.co.uk/bhimani**

Contents

The table below explains which solution pertains to which question paper. Answers not shown are on the website.

Question	Question Paper	Topics covered	Answer page
1	June 2005 (Question 3)	**Variance Analysis & Standard Costing**	**69**
2	June 2005 (Question 5)	**JIT**	**72**
3	June 2005 (Question 3)	**Strategy**	**75**
4	June 2005 (Question 4)	**CVP Analysis and Performance**	
5	May 2005 (Question 1)	**CVP Analysis**	
6	May 2005 (Question 2a)	**Balance Scorecard**	
7	May 2005 (Question 3)	**ABC Costing**	
8	November 2005 (Question 1)	**ABC Costing**	
9	November 2005 (Question 2b)	**Variance Analysis**	
10	November 2005 (Question 3)	**Process Accounting**	
11	November 2005 (Question 4)	**Performance Evaluation**	
12	May 2006 (Question 3)	**Budget & Variance Analysis**	
13	May 2006 (Question 4)	**Transaction Cost**	
14	November 2006 (Question 1)	**Variance Analysis**	
15	November 2006 (Question 4)	**Transaction Cost**	
16	Pilot Paper May 2004 (Question 4)	**Process Accounting**	
17	Pilot Paper May 2005 (Question 3)	**Project Evaluation (Incremental Analysis)**	
18	Pilot Paper May 2005 (Question 5)	**Project Evaluation (Incremental Analysis)**	
19	Pilot Paper May 2005 (Question 6a)	**Relevant Costs**	
20	Pilot Paper May 2005 (Question 7b)	**CVP Analysis**	
21	Pilot Paper November 2005 (Question 3)	**Absorption Costing VS Variable Costing**	

22	Pilot Paper November 2005 (Question 5)	**Project Evaluation**	
23	Pilot Paper November 2005 (Question 7)	**ABC Costing**	
24	Pilot Paper May 2006 (Question 2)	**Sensitivity Analysis**	
25	Pilot Paper May 2006 (Question 7)	**CVP Analysis**	
26	Pilot Paper November 2006 (Question 2)	**Value Chain Analysis**	
27	Pilot Paper November 2006 (Question 4)	**CVP Analysis**	
28	Pilot Paper November 2006 (Question 5)	**ABC Costing**	
29	Pilot Paper November 2006 (Question 6)	**Incremental Analysis**	
30	Pilot Paper November 2006 (Question 7)	**Project Evaluation**	
31	2005 (Question 2)	**Budgeting**	
32	2006 (Question 2)	**Budgeting**	
33	2006 (Question 3)	**CVP Analysis**	

1

Question 3 – June 2005, ACCA

BRK Co operates an absorption costing system and sells three products, B, R and K which are substitutes for each other. The following standard selling price and cost data relate to these three products:

Product	Selling price per unit	Direct material per unit	Direct labour per unit
B	£14.00	3.00 kg at £1.80 per kg	0.5 hrs at £6.50 per hr
R	£15.00	1.25 kg at £3·28 per kg	0·8 hrs at £6·50 per hr
K	£18·00	1·94 kg at £2·50 per kg	0·7 hrs at £6·50 per hr

Budgeted fixed production overhead for the last period was £81,000. This was absorbed on a machine hour basis. The standard machine hours for each product and the budgeted levels of production and sales for each product for the last period are as follows:

Product	B	R	K
Standard machine hours per unit	0·3 hrs	0·6 hrs	0·8 hrs
Budgeted production and sales (units)	10,000	13,000	9,000

Actual volumes and selling prices for the three products in the last period are as follows:

Product	B	R	K
Actual selling price per unit	£14·50	£15·50	£19·00
Actual production and sales (units)	9,500	13,500	8,500

Required:

(a) Calculate the following variances for overall sales for the last period:

    (i) sales price variance;

    (ii) sales volume profit variance;

    (iii) sales mix profit variance;

    (iv) sales quantity profit variance

    and reconcile budgeted profit for the period to actual sales less standard cost.

(13 marks)

(b) Discuss the significance of the sales mix profit variance and comment on whether any useful information would be obtained by calculating mix variances for each of these three products.   (4 marks)

(c) Describe the essential elements of a standard costing system and explain how quantitative analysis can assist in the preparation of standard costs.   (8 marks)

(25 marks)

© ACCA

2

Question 5 – June 2005, ACCA

TNG Co expects the annual demand for product X to be 255,380 units. Product X has a selling price of £19 per unit and is purchased for £11 per unit from a supplier, MKR Co. TNG places an order for 50,000 units of product X at regular intervals throughout the year. Because the demand for product X is to some degree uncertain, TNG maintains a safety (buffer) stock of product X which is sufficient to meet the demand for 28 working days. The cost of placing an order is £25 and the storage cost for Product X is 10 pence per unit per year.

TNG normally pays trade suppliers after 60 days, but MKR has offered a discount of 1% for cash settlement within 20 days.

TNG Co has a short-term cost of debt of 8% and uses a working year consisting of 365 days.

Required:

(a) Calculate the annual cost of the current ordering policy. Ignore financing costs in this part of the question. (4 marks)

(b) Calculate the annual saving if the economic order quantity model is used to determine an optimal ordering policy. Ignore financing costs in this part of the question. (5 marks)

(c) Determine whether the discount offered by the supplier is financially acceptable to TNG Co. (4 marks)

(d) Critically discuss the limitations of the economic order quantity model as a way of managing stock. (4 marks)

(e) Discuss the advantages and disadvantages of using just-in-time stock management methods. (8 marks)

(25 marks)

© ACCA

3

Question 3 – June 2005, ACCA

Better budgeting in recent years may have been seen as a movement from 'incremental budgeting' to alternative budgeting approaches. However, academic studies (e.g. Beyond Budgeting – Hope & Fraser) argue that the annual budget model may be seen as (i) having a number of inherent weaknesses and (ii) acting as a barrier to the effective implementation of alternative models for use in the accomplishment of strategic change.

Required:

(a) Identify and comment on FIVE inherent weaknesses of the annual budget model irrespective of the budgeting approach that is applied. (8 marks)

(b) Discuss ways in which the traditional budgeting process may be seen as a barrier to the achievement of the aims of EACH of the following models for the implementation of strategic change:

   (i)   benchmarking;

   (ii) balanced scorecard;

   (iii) activity-based models. (12 marks)

(20 marks)

© ACCA

4

Question 4 – June 2005, ACCA

CVP Analysis and Performance

The Dental Health Partnership was established in 1992 and provides dentistry and other related services to the population of Blaintopia, a country in which the public health service is partially funded by the Government. Additional information relating to the Dental Health Partnership for the year ended 31 May 2005 is as follows:

1. The partnership was open for 5 days per week during 48 weeks of the year.

2. Each dentist treated 20 patients per day. The maximum number of patients that could have been treated by a dentist on any working day was 24 patients.

3. (i) The partnership received a payment from the government each time any patient was consulted as shown in the following table:

Category of treatment	Payments from government ($£$)
No treatment required	12
Minor treatment	50
Major treatment	100

   (ii) In addition, adult patients paid a fee for each consultation which was equal to the amount of the payment shown per category of treatment in the above table. Children and senior citizens were not required to pay a fee for any dental consultations.

4. The partnership received an annual fee of $£20,800$ from a well-known manufacturer of dental products under a fixed-term contract of three years' duration. The contract commenced on 1 June 2004 and relates to the promotion of the products of the manufacturer.

5. The total of material and consumable costs (which are 100% variable) during the year ended 31 May 2005 amounted to $£446,400$.

6. Staff costs were paid as follows:

Category of employee	Salary/annum per employee (£)
Dentist	60,000
Dental assistant	20,000
Administrator	16,000

Note: A fixed bonus payment amounting to 4% of their basic salary was paid to each Dental Assistant and Administrator.

7. Establishment costs and other operating costs amounted to £85,000 and £75,775 respectively for the year ended 31 May 2005.

8. All costs other than materials and consumables costs incurred by the Dental Health Partnership are subject to contracts and are therefore to be treated as fixed costs.

9. A table of non-financial information relating to the Dental Health Partnership for the year ended 31 May 2005 is as follows:

Number of dentists	6
Dental assistants	7
Administrators	2
Patient 'mix' (%):	
Adults	50
Children	40
Senior citizens	10
Mix of patient appointments (%):	
No treatment required	70
Minor treatment	20
Major treatment	10

Required:

(a) Prepare a summary Profit and Loss Account of the Dental Health Partnership for the year ended 31 May 2005 and calculate the percentage of maximum capacity that was required to be utilised in order to break even in the year ended 31 May 2005. (12 marks)

(b) Discuss FOUR factors that distinguish service from manufacturing organisations and explain how each of these factors relates to the services provided by the Dental Health Partnership. (5 marks)

(c) Excluding the number of complaints by patients, identify and briefly explain THREE quantitative non-financial performance measures that could be used to assess the 'quality of service' provided by the Dental Health Partnership.

(3 marks)

(20 marks)

© ACCA

5

Question 1.14-1.16 – May 2005, CIMA Professional Paper P1

SM makes two products, Z1 and Z2. Its machines can work only on one product at a time. The two products are worked on in two departments by differing grades of labour. The labour requirements for the two products are as follows:

Minutes per unit of product

	Z1	Z2
Department 1	12	16
Department 2	20	15

There is currently a shortage of labour and the maximum times available each day in Departments 1 and 2 are 480 minutes and 840 minutes, respectively. The current selling prices and costs for the two products are shown below:

	Z1	Z2
	£ per unit	£ per unit
Selling price	50.00	65.00
Direct materials	10.00	15.00
Direct labour	10.40	6.20
Variable overheads	6.40	9.20
Fixed overheads	12.80	18.40
Profit per unit	10.40	16.20

As part of the budget-setting process, SM needs to know the optimum output levels. All output is sold.

Required:

1.14 Calculate the maximum number of each product that could be produced each day and identify the limiting factor/bottleneck. (3 marks)

1.15 Using traditional contribution analysis, calculate the 'profit-maximising' output each day and the contribution at this level of output. (3 marks)

1.16 Using a throughput approach, calculate the 'throughput-maximising' output each day and the 'throughput contribution' at this level of output.   (3 marks)

(9 marks)

© CIMA

6

Question 2(a) – May 2005, CIMA Professional Paper P1

A general insurance company is about to implement a Balanced Scorecard. You are required to

(i) State the four perspectives of a Balanced Scorecard; and

(ii) Recommend one performance measure that would be appropriate for a general insurance company, for each of the four perspectives, and give a reason to support each measure. (You must recommend one measure only for each perspective. (5 marks)

(5 marks)

© CIMA

7

Question 3 – May 2005, CIMA Professional Paper P1

F plc supplies pharmaceutical drugs to drug stores. Although the company makes a satisfactory return, the directors are concerned that some orders are profitable and others are not. The management has decided to investigate a new budgeting system using activity-based costing principles to ensure that all orders they accept are making a profit.

Each customer order is charged as follows. Customers are charged the list price of the drugs ordered plus a charge for selling and distribution costs (overheads). A profit margin is also added, but that does not form part of this analysis.

Currently F plc uses a simple absorption rate to absorb these overheads. The rate is calculated based on the budgeted annual selling and distribution costs and the budgeted annual total list price of the drugs ordered.

An analysis of customers has revealed that many customers place frequent small orders with each order requesting a variety of drugs. The management of F plc has examined more carefully the nature of its selling and distribution costs, and the following data have been prepared for the budget for next year:

Total list price of drugs supplied	£8 million
Number of customer orders	8,000

Selling and distribution costs	£000	Cost driver
Invoice processing	280	See Note 2
Packing	220	Size of package – see Note 3
Delivery	180	Number of deliveries – see Note 4
Other overheads	200	Number of orders
Total overheads	880	

Notes:

1. Each order will be shipped in one package and will result in one delivery to the customer and one invoice (an order never results in more than one delivery).

2. Each invoice has a different line for each drug ordered. There are 28,000 invoice lines each year. It is estimated that 25% of invoice processing costs are related to the number of invoices and 75% are related to the number of invoice lines.

3. Packing costs are £32 for a large package and £25 for a small package.

4. The delivery vehicles are always filled to capacity for each journey. The delivery vehicles can carry either 6 large packages or 12 small packages (or appropriate combinations of large and small packages). It is estimated that there will be 1,000 delivery journeys each year, and the total delivery mileage that is specific to particular customers is estimated at 350,000 miles each year. £40,000 of delivery costs are related to loading the delivery vehicles and the remainder of these costs are related to specific delivery distance to customers.

The management has asked for two typical orders to be costed using next year's budget data, using the current method, and the proposed activity-based costing approach. Details of two typical orders are shown below:

	Order A	Order B
Lines on invoice	2	8
Package size	Small	Large
Specific delivery distance (miles)	8	40
List price of drugs supplied (£)	1,200	900

Required:

(a) Calculate the charge for selling and distribution overheads for Order A and Order B using

    (i) the current system; and

    (ii) the activity-based costing approach.   (10 marks)

(b) Write a report to the management of F plc in which you

    (i) assess the strengths and weaknesses of the proposed activity-based costing approach for F plc; and   (5 marks)

(ii) recommend the actions that the management of F plc might consider in light of the data produced using the activity-based costing approach.   (5 marks)

(20 marks)

© CIMA

8

Question 1.14-1.16 – November 2005, CIMA Professional Paper P1

K makes many products, one of which is Product Z. K is considering adopting an activity-based costing approach for setting its budget, in place of the current practice of absorbing overheads using direct labour hours. The main budget categories and cost driver details for the whole company for October are set out below, excluding direct material costs:

Budget category	£	Cost driver details
Direct labour	128,000	8,000 direct labour hours
Set-up costs	22,000	88 set-ups each month
Quality testing costs*	34,000	40 tests each month
Other overhead costs	32,000	Absorbed by direct labour hours

*A quality test is performed after every 75 units produced

The following data for Product Z is provided:

Direct materials	budgeted cost of £21.50 per unit
Direct labour	budgeted at 0.3 hours per unit
Batch size	30 units
Set-ups	2 set-ups per batch
Budgeted volume for October	150 units

Required:

1.14 Calculate the budgeted unit cost of product Z for October assuming that a direct labour-based absorption method was used for all overheads.   (2 marks)

1.15 Calculate the budgeted unit cost of product Z for October using an activity-based costing approach.   (3 marks)

Management & Cost Accounting: Professional Exam Questions.
© Pearson Education Limited 2008

1.16 Explain in less than 50 words, why the costs absorbed by a product using an activity-based costing approach could be higher than those absorbed if a traditional labour-based absorption system were used, and identify two implications of this for management. (4 marks)

(9 marks)

© CIMA

9

Question 2(b) – November 2005, CIMA Professional Paper P1

An analysis of past output has shown that batches have a mean weight of 90 kg and that the weights conform to the normal distribution with a standard deviation of 10 kg. The company has a policy to investigate variances that fall outside the range that includes 95% of the outcomes. In September one sample batch weighed 110 kg.

Required:

(i) Calculate whether the material usage variance for this batch should be investigated according to the company policy described above. (3 marks)

(ii) Discuss two other important factors that should be taken into account when deciding whether to investigate this variance. (2 marks)

(5 marks)

© CIMA

10

Question 3 – November 2005, CIMA Professional Paper P1

(a) M Pty produces 'Biotinct' in a lengthy distillation and cooling process. Base materials are introduced at the start of this process, and further chemicals are added when it is 80% complete. Each kilogram of base materials produces 1 kg of Biotinct.

Data for October are

Opening work in process	40 kg of base materials, 25% processed	
Cost of opening work in process	Base materials	$1,550
	Processing	$ 720
Costs incurred in October	Base materials (80 kg)	$3,400
	Conversion costs	$6,864
	Further chemicals	$7,200
Closing work in process	50 kg of base materials, 90% processed	
Finished output	65 kg of Biotinct	

Under normal conditions there are no losses of base materials in this process. However, in October, 5 kg of partially complete Biotinct were spoiled immediately after further chemicals had been added. The 5 kg of spoiled Biotinct was not processed to finished goods stage and was sold for a total of $200.

Required:

Using the FIFO method prepare the process account for October.   (12 marks)

(b) One of the company's management accountants overheard the Managing Director arguing as follows, "These process accounts are complicated to produce, and often conceal the true position. As I see it, the value of partly processed Biotinct is zero. In October we spent $17,464 and the output was 65 kg. So the average cost was $268·68 per kilogram, while the target cost is $170 ($40 for base materials, $70 for processing and $60 for further chemicals). These figures make me concerned about production efficiency."

Required:

Explain to the Managing Director any errors in the comment he had made, and discuss whether the data from the process account indicate that there has been production inefficiency. (8 marks)

(20 marks)

© CIMA

11

Question 4 – November 2005, CIMA Professional Paper P1

Y and Z are two divisions of a large company that operate in similar markets. The divisions are treated as investment centres and every month they each prepare an operating statement to be submitted to the parent company. Operating statements for these two divisions for October are shown below:

Operating statements for October

	Y	Z
	£000	£000
Sales revenue	900	555
Less variable costs	345	312
Contribution	555	243
Less controllable fixed costs	95	42
(includes depreciation on divisional assets)		
Controllable income	460	201
Less apportioned central costs	338	180
Net income before tax	122	21
Total divisional net assets	£9.76 million	£1.26 million

The company currently has a target return on capital of 12% per annum. However, the company believes its cost of capital is likely to rise and is considering increasing the target return on capital. At present the performance of each division and the divisional management is assessed primarily on the basis of return on investment (ROI).

Required:

(a) Calculate the annualised return on investment (ROI) for divisions Y and Z, and discuss the relative performance of the two divisions using the ROI data and other information given above.

(9 marks)

(b) Calculate the annualised residual income (RI) for divisions Y and Z, and explain the implications of this information for the evaluation of the divisions' performance. (6 marks)

(c) Briefly discuss the strengths and weaknesses of ROI and RI as methods of assessing the performance of divisions. Explain two further methods of assessment of divisional performance that could be used in addition to ROI or RI. (5 marks)

(20 marks)

© CIMA

12

Question 3 – May 2006, CIMA Professional Paper P1

M plc designs' manufactures and assembles furniture. The furniture is for home use and therefore varies considerably in size, complexity and value. One of the departments in the company is the Assembly Department. This department is labour intensive; the workers travel to various locations to assemble and fit the furniture using the packs of finished timbers that have been sent to them.

Budgets are set centrally and they are then given to the managers of the various departments who then have the responsibility of achieving their respective targets. Actual costs are compared against the budgets and the managers are then asked to comment on the budgetary control statement. The statement for April for the Assembly Department is shown below:

	Budget	**Actual**	**Variance**
Assembly labour hours	6,400	7,140	
	$	$	$
Assembly labour	51,970	58,227	6,257 Adverse
Furniture packs	224,000	205,000	19,000 Favourable
Other materials	23,040	24,100	1,060 Adverse
Overheads	62,060	112,340	50,280 Adverse
Total	361,070	399,667	38,597 Adverse

Note: the costs shown are for assembling and fitting the furniture (they do not include time spent travelling to jobs and the related costs). The hours worked by the Manager are not included in the figure given for the assembly labour hours.

The Manager of the Assembly Department is new to the job and has very little previous experience of working with budgets but he does have many years' experience as a supervisor in assembly departments. Based on that experience he was sure that the department had performed well. He has asked for your help in replying to a memo which he has just received asking him to "explain the serious overspending in his department". He has sent you some additional information about the budget:

1. The budgeted and actual assembly labour costs include the fixed salary of $2,050 for the Manager of the Assembly Department. All of the other labour is paid for the hours they work.

2. The cost of furniture packs and other materials is assumed by the central finance office of M plc to vary in proportion to the number of assembly labour hours worked.

3. The budgeted overhead costs are made up of three elements: a fixed cost of $9,000 for services from central headquarters, a stepped fixed cost which changes when the assembly hours exceed 7,000 hours, and some variable overheads. The variable overheads are assumed to vary in proportion to the number of assembly labour hours. Working papers for the budget showed the impact on the overhead costs of differing amounts of assembly labour hours:

Assembly labour hours	5,000	7,500	10,000
Overhead costs	$54,500	$76,500	$90,000

The actual fixed costs for April were as budgeted.

Required:

(a) Prepare, using the additional information that the Manager of the Assembly Department has given you, a budgetary control statement that would be more helpful to him. (7 marks)

(b) (i) Discuss the differences between the format of the statement that you have produced and that is supplied by M plc. (4 marks)

    (ii) Discuss the assumption made by the central office of M plc that costs vary in proportion to assembly labour hours. (3 marks)

(c) Discuss whether M plc should change to a system of participative budgeting.

(6 marks)

(20 marks)

© CIMA

13

Question 4 – May 2006, CIMA Professional Paper P1

FP sells and repairs photocopiers. The company has operated for many years with two departments, the Sales Department and the Service Department, but the departments had no autonomy. The company is now thinking of restructuring so that the two departments will become profit centres.

The Sales Department

This department sells new photocopiers. The department sells 2,000 copiers per year. Included in the selling price is £60 for a one year guarantee. All customers pay this fee. This means that during the first year of ownership if the photocopier needs to be repaired then the repair costs are not charged to the customer. On average, 500 photocopiers per year need to be repaired under the guarantee. The repair work is carried out by the Service Department who, under the proposed changes, would charge the Sales Department for doing the repairs. It is estimated that on average the repairs will take 3 hours each and that the charge by the Service Department will be £136,500 for the 500 repairs.

The Service Department

This department has two sources of work: the work needed to satisfy the guarantees for the Sales Department and repair work for external customers. Customers are charged at full cost plus 40%. The details of the budget for the next year for the Service Department revealed standard costs of

Parts	Cost (£)
Labour	15 per hour
Variable overheads	10 per labour hour
Fixed overheads	22 per labour hour

The calculation of these standards is based on the estimated maximum market demand and includes the expected 500 repairs for the Sales Department. The average cost of the parts needed for a repair is £54. This means that the charge to

Management & Cost Accounting: Professional Exam Questions.
© Pearson Education Limited 2008

the Sales Department for the repair work, including the 40% mark-up, will be £136,500.

Proposed Change

It has now been suggested that FP should be structured so that the two departments become profit centres and that the managers of the Departments are given autonomy. The individual salaries of the managers would be linked to the profits of their respective departments.

Budgets have been produced for each department on the assumption that the Service Department will repair 500 photocopiers for the Sales Department and that the transfer price for this work will be calculated in the same way as the price charged to external customers.

However the manager of the Sales Department has now stated that he intends to have the repairs done by another company, RS, because they have offered to carry out the work for a fixed fee of £180 per repair and this is less than the price that the Sales Department would charge.

Required:

(a) Calculate the individual profits of the Sales Department and the Service Department, and of FP as a whole from the guarantee scheme if:

   (i) the repairs are carried out by the Service Department and are charged at full cost plus 40%;

   (ii) the repairs are carried out by the Service department and are charged at marginal cost;

   (iii) the repairs are carried out by RS.   **(8 marks)**

(b) (i) Explain, with reasons, why a 'full cost plus' transfer pricing model may not be appropriate for FP.   **(3 marks)**

   (ii) Comment on other issues that the managers of FP should consider if they decide to allow RS to carry out the repairs.   **(4 marks)**

(c) Briefly explain the advantages and disadvantages of structuring the departments as profit centres.   **(5 marks)**

(20 marks)

© CIMA

14

Question 1.1-1.6 – November 2006, CIMA Professional Paper P1

The following data are given for sub-questions 1.1 to 1.3 below.

A company uses standard absorption costing. The following information was recorded by the company for October:

	Budget	Actual
Output and sales (units)	8,700	8,200
Selling price per unit (£)	26	31
Variable cost per unit (£)	10	10
Total fixed overheads (£)	34,800	37,000

1.1   The sales price variance for October was

(A) £38,500 favourable

(B) £41,000 favourable

(C) £41,000 adverse

(D) £65,600 adverse. (2 marks)

1.2   The sales volume profit variance for October was

(A) £6,000 adverse

(B) £6,000 favourable

(C) £8,000 adverse

(D) £8,000 favourable. (2 marks)

1.3   The fixed overhead volume variance for October was

(A) £2,000 adverse

(B) £2,200 adverse

(C) £2,200 favourable

(D) £4,200 adverse. (2 marks)

1.4   A master budget comprises the

(A) budgeted income statement and budgeted cash flow only.

(B) budgeted income statement and budgeted balance sheet only.

(C) budgeted income statement and budgeted capital expenditure only.

(D) budgeted income statement, budgeted balance sheet and budgeted cash flow only.

(2 marks)

The annual operating statement for a company is shown below:

	£000
Sales revenue	800
Less variable costs	390
Contribution	410
Less fixed costs	90
Less depreciation	20
Net income	300
Assets	£6.75 million

The cost of capital is 13% per annum.

Required:

1.5   The return on investment (ROI) for the company is closest to

(A) 4.44%

(B) 4.74%

(C) 5.77%

(D) 6.07%   (2 marks)

1.6   The residual income (RI) for the company is closest to

£000

(A) (467)

(B) (487)

(C) (557)

(D) (577)   (2 marks)

Question 1.1-1.6 – November 2006, CIMA Professional Paper P1

X Ltd has two production departments, Assembly and Finishing, and two service departments, Stores and Maintenance.

Stores department provides the following service to the production departments: 60% to Assembly and 40% to Finishing.

Maintenance provides the following service to the production and service departments:

40% to Assembly, 45% to Finishing and 15% to Stores.

The budgeted information for the year is as follows:

Budgeted fixed production overheads

	£
Assembly	100,000
Finishing	150,000
Stores	50,000
Maintenance	40,000
Budgeted output	100,000 units

At the end of the year after apportioning the service department overheads, the total fixed production overheads debited to the Assembly department's fixed production overhead control account were £180,000.

The actual output achieved was 120,000 units.

Required:

Calculate the under/over absorption of fixed production overheads for the Assembly department. (4 marks)

© CIMA

15

Question 4 – November 2006, CIMA Professional Paper P1

The ZZ Group has two divisions, X and Y. Each division produces only one type of product: X produces a component (C) and Y produces a finished product (FP). Each FP needs one C. It is the current policy of the group for C to be transferred to Division Y at the marginal cost of £10 per component and that Y must buy all the components it needs from X.

The markets for the component and the finished product are competitive and price sensitive. Component C is produced by many other companies but it is thought that the external demand for the next year could increase to 1,000 units more than the sales volume shown in the current budget for Division X.

Budgeted data, taken from the ZZ Group Internal Information System, for the divisions for the next year is as follows:

Division X

Income statement

Sales (£)	70,000
Cost of sales	
Variable costs (£)	50,000
Contribution (£)	20,000
Fixed costs (controllable) (£)	15,000
Profit (£)	5,000
Production/Sales (units)	5,000 (3,000 of which are transferred to Division Y)
External demand (units)	3,000 (Only 2,000 of which can be currently satisfied)
Capacity (units)	5,000
External market price per unit	£20

Balance sheet extract

Capital employed   £60,000

Other information

Cost of capital charge   10%

Division Y

Income statement

Sales (£)	270,000
Cost of sales	
Variable costs (£)	114,000
Contribution (£)	156,000
Fixed costs (controllable) (£)	100,000
Profit (£)	56,000
Production/Sales (units)	3,000
Capacity (units)	7,000
Market price per unit	£90

Balance sheet extract

Capital employed (£)   110,000

Other information

Cost of capital charge   10%

Four measures are used to evaluate the performance of the Divisional Managers. Based on the data above, the budgeted performance measures for the two divisions are as follows:

	Division X	Division Y
Residual income (£)	(1,000)	45,000
Return on capital employed (%)	8.33	50.91
Operating profit margin (%)	7.14	20.74
Asset turnover	1.17	2.46

Current policy

It is the current policy of the group for C to be transferred to Division Y at the marginal cost of £10 per component and that Y must buy all the components that it needs from X.

Proposed policy

ZZ Group is thinking of giving the Divisional Managers the freedom to set their own transfer price and to buy the components from external suppliers but there are concerns about problemsthat could arise by granting such autonomy.

Required:

(a) If the transfer price of the component is set by the Manager of Division X at the current market price (£20 per component), recalculate the budgeted performance measures for each division. (8 marks)

(b) Discuss the changes to the performance measures of the divisions that would arise as a result of altering the transfer price to £20 per component. (6 marks)

(c) (i) Explain the problems that could arise for each of the Divisional Managers and for ZZ Group as a whole as a result of giving full autonomy to the Divisional Managers.

   (ii) Discuss how the problems you have explained could be resolved without resorting to a policy of imposed transfer prices. (6 marks)

(20 marks)

© CIMA

16

Question 4 – CIMA P1 Pilot Paper

PQR plc is a chemical processing company. The company produces a range of solvents by passing materials through a series of processes. The company uses the First In First Out (FIFO) valuation method.

In Process 2, the output from Process 1 (XP1) is blended with two other materials (P2A and P2B) to form XP2. It is expected that 10% of any new input to Process 2 (that is, transfers from Process 1 plus Process 2 materials added) will be immediately lost and that this loss will have no resale value. It is also expected that in addition to the loss, 5% of any new input will form a by-product, Z, which can be sold without additional processing for £2.00 per litre.

Data from Process 2 for November 2003 is as follows:

Opening work in process

Process 2 had 1,200 litres of opening work in process. The value and degree of completion of this was as follows:

	£	Degree of completion (%)
XP1	1,560	100
P2A	1,540	100
P2B	750	100
Conversion costs	3,790	40
	7,640	

Input

During November, the inputs to Process 2 were as follows:

		£
XP1	5,000 litres	15,679
P2A	1,200 litres	6,000
P2B	3,000 litres	4,500
Conversion costs		22,800

Closing work in process

At the end of November, the work in process was 1,450 litres. This was fully complete in respect of all materials, but only 30% complete for conversion costs.

Output

The output from Process 2 during November was as follows:

Z   460 litres

XP2   7,850 litres

Required:

Prepare the Process 2 account for November 2003.   (17 marks)

Note: 3 marks will be awarded for presentation.

(20 marks)

© CIMA

17

Question 3 – May 2005, CIMA Professional Paper P2

A company is considering the replacement of its delivery vehicle. It has chosen the vehicle that it will acquire but it now needs to decide whether the vehicle should be purchased or leased.

The cost of the vehicle is £15,000. If the company purchases the vehicle, it will be entitled to claim tax depreciation at the rate of 25% per year on a reducing balance basis. The vehicle is expected to have a trade-in value of £5,000 at the end of three years.

If the company leases the vehicle, it will make an initial payment of £1,250 plus annual payments of £4,992 at the end of each of three years. The full value of each lease payment will be an allowable cost in the computation of the company's taxable profits of the year in which the payments are made.

The company pays corporation tax at the rate of 30% of its profits.

Out of this, 50% of the tax is payable in the year in which profits are made and 50% in the following year. Assume that the company has sufficient profits to obtain tax relief on its acquisition of the vehicle in accordance with the information provided above.

The company's after tax cost of capital is 15% per year.

Note: Tax depreciation is not a cash cost but is allowed as a deduction in the calculation of taxable profits.

Required:

Calculate whether the company should purchase or lease the vehicle and clearly state your recommendation to the company.   (10 marks)

© CIMA

18

Question 5 – May 2005, CIMA Professional Paper P2

A printing company is considering investing in new equipment which has a capital cost of £3 million. The machine qualifies for tax depreciation at the rate of 25% per year on a reducing balance basis and has an expected life of five years. The residual value of the machine is expected to be £300,000 at the end of five years.

An existing machine would be sold immediately for £400,000 if a new machine were to be bought. This existing machine has a tax written down value of £250,000.

The existing machine generates annual revenues of £4 million and earns a contribution of 40% of sales. The new machine would reduce unit variable costs to 80% of their former value and increase output capacity by 20%. There is sufficient sales demand at the existing prices to make full use of this additional capacity.

The printing company pays corporation tax on its profits at the rate of 30%, with half of the tax being payable in the year that the profit is earned and half in the following year.

The company's after tax cost of capital is 14% per year.

Required:

(a) Evaluate the proposed purchase of the new printing machine from a financial perspective using appropriate calculations, and advise the company as to whether the investment is worthwhile. (15 marks)

(b) Explain sensitivity analysis and prepare calculations to show the sensitivity of the decision to independent changes in each of the following:

    (i) annual contribution;

    (ii) rate of corporation tax on profits. (10 marks)

(25 marks)

© CIMA

19

Question 6(a) – May 2005, CIMA Professional Paper P2

The CS group is planning its annual marketing conference for its sales executives and has approached the VBJ Holiday company (VBJ) to obtain a quotation.

VBJ has been trying to win the business of the CS group for some time and is keen to provide a quotation which the CS group will find acceptable in the hope that this will lead to future contracts.

The manager of VBJ has produced the following cost estimate for the conference:

	$
Coach running costs	2,000
Driver costs	3,000
Hotel costs	5,000
General overheads	2,000
Sub-total	12,000
Profit (30%)	3,600
Total	15,600

You have considered this cost estimate but you believe that it would be more appropriate to base the quotation on relevant costs. You have therefore obtained the following further information:

Coach running costs represent the fuel costs of $1,500 plus an apportionment of the annual fixed costs of operating the coach. No specific fixed costs would be incurred if the coach is used on this contract. If the contract did not go ahead, the coach would not be in use for eight out of the ten days of the conference. For the other two days a contract has already been accepted which contains a significant financial penalty clause. This contract earns a contribution of $250 per day. A replacement coach could be hired for $180 per day.

Driver costs represent the salary and related employment costs of one driver for 10 days. If a driver is used on this contract, the company will need to replace the driver so that VBJ can complete its existing work. The replacement driver would be hired from a recruitment agency that charges $400 per day for a suitably qualified driver.

Hotel costs are the expected costs of hiring the hotel for the conference.

General overheads are based upon the overhead absorption rate of VBJ and are set annually when the company prepares its budgets. The only general overhead cost that can be specifically identified with the conference is the time that has been spent in considering the costs of the conference and preparing the quotation. This amounted to $250.

Required:

Prepare a statement showing the total relevant cost of the contract. Explain clearly the reasons for each of the values in your quotation and for excluding any of the costs (if appropriate). (10 marks)

© CIMA

20

Question 7(b) – May 2005, CIMA Professional Paper P2

Market research has discovered that the price demand relationship for the item during the initial launch phase will be as follows:

Price (£)	Demand (units)
100	10,000
80	20,000
69	30,000
62	40,000

Production of the DVD recorder would occur in batches of 10,000 units, and the production director believes that 50% of the variable manufacturing cost would be affected by a learning and experience curve. This would apply to each batch produced and continue at a constant rate of learning up to a production volume of 40,000 units when the learning would be complete.

Thereafter, the unit variable manufacturing cost of the product would be equal to the unit cost of the fourth batch. The production director estimates that the unit variable manufacturing cost of the first batch would be £60 (£30 of which is subject to the effect of the learning and experience curve, and £30 of which is unaffected), whereas the average unit variable manufacturing cost of all four batches would be £52.71.

There are no non-manufacturing variable costs associated with the DVD recorder.

Required:

(i) Calculate the rate of learning that is expected by the production director.

(4 marks)

(ii) Calculate the optimum price at which Q should sell the DVD recorder in order to maximise its profits during the initial launch phase of the product. (8 marks)

(iii) Q expects that after the initial launch phase the market price will be £57 per unit. Estimated product-specific fixed costs during this phase of the product's life are expected to be £15,000 per month. During this phase of the product's life cycle, Q wishes to achieve a target monthly profit from the product of £30,000. Calculate the number of units that need to be sold each month during this phase in order that Q achieves this target monthly profit. (3 marks)

(15 marks)

© CIMA

21

Question 3 – November 2005, CIMA Professional Paper P2

ML is an engineering company that specialises in providing engineering facilities to businesses that cannot justify operating their own facilities in-house. ML employs a number of engineers who are skilled in different engineering techniques that enable ML to provide a full range of engineering facilities to its customers. Most of the work undertaken by ML is unique to each of its customers, often requiring the manufacture of spare parts for its customers' equipment or the building of new equipment from customer drawings. As a result, most of ML's work is short term, with some jobs being completed within hours while others may take a few days.

To date ML has adopted a cost plus approach for setting its prices. This is based upon an absorption costing system that uses machine hours as the basis of absorbing overhead costs into individual job costs. The Managing Director is concerned that over recent months ML has been unsuccessful when quoting for work with the consequence that there has been an increase in the level of unused capacity. It has been suggested that ML should adopt an alternative approach to its pricing based on marginal costing, since "any price that exceeds variable costs is better than no work".

Required:

With reference to the above scenario,

(i) briefly explain absorption and marginal cost approaches to pricing;

(ii) discuss the validity of the comment "any price that exceeds variable costs is better than no work". (10 marks)

© CIMA

22

Question 5 – November 2005, CIMA Professional Paper P2

The MP Organisation is an independent film production company. It has a number of potential films that it is considering producing, one of which is the subject of a management meeting next week. The film which has been code named CA45 is a thriller based on a novel by a well respected author.

The script has already been written at a cost of $10,000 and preliminary discussions have been held with the lead actors. The MP Organisation has incurred travel and other incidental costs of $4,000 to date. The following additional costs have been estimated in order to produce the film:

	$000
Production director's fee	100
Set design	10
Costumes and wardrobe	20
Actors' fees	50
Musician/songwriter for soundtrack	5
Camera and equipment hire	20
Actors' travel and accommodation costs	10
Other production costs	5

Production of the film is estimated to take 16 weeks, and all of the above costs would be incurred during this period, though there is some uncertainty about the accuracy of these cost estimates. These cost values are those most likely to be incurred. With the exception of the payment to the production director which is a fixed fee, the other costs could be up to 10% higher or lower than the values estimated.

In addition there will be advertising, promotion and marketing costs of $15,000 immediately, $10,000 in each of years 1 and 2, and then $5,000 during each of the next three years. These figures are not subject to any uncertainty.

The film is expected to have a life of five years. During the first three years the film will be sold to cinemas through distributors and MP will receive 25% of the gross revenues. The film will be sold as a DVD for the remaining two years and MP will receive 100% of these revenues. The expected gross revenues are as follows:

Year	Source	Gross revenue ($)	MP's share (%)
1	Cinema	400,000	25
2	Cinema	600,000	25
3	Cinema	450,000	25
4	DVD	50,000	100
5	DVD	30,000	100

However, it is thought that the gross revenues could vary by as much as 20% higher or lower than those stated, depending on the popularity of the film. The initial level of popularity will continue for all five years.

The MP Organisation evaluates new films using a cost of capital of 15% per year.

Required:

(a) Prepare calculations for each combination of the most likely, optimistic and pessimistic cost and revenue values to evaluate whether or not the MP Organisation should continue with the production of the film. Discuss your analysis and make a recommendation to MP.   (15 marks)

(b) Prepare notes for the management meeting that explain how probabilities can be used

   (i) to calculate the expected NPV; and

   (ii) in a simulation model to evaluate the risk of a long-term decision.

                                                              (10 marks)

                                                              (25 marks)

© CIMA

23

Question 7 – November 2005, CIMA Professional Paper P2

ZP plc is a marketing consultancy that provides marketing advice and support to small and medium sized enterprises. ZP plc employs four full-time marketing consultants, each of whom is expected to deliver 1,500 chargeable hours per year and receive a salary of £60,000 per year. In addition the company employs six marketing support/administration staff whose combined total salary cost is £120,000 per year.

ZP plc has estimated its other costs for the coming year as follows:

	£000
Office premises: rent, rates, heating	50
Advertising	5
Travel to clients	15
Accommodation whilst visiting clients	11
Telephone, fax, communications	10

ZP plc has been attributing costs to each client (and to the projects undertaken for them) by recording the chargeable hours spent on each client and using a single cost rate of £75 per chargeable hour. The same basis has been used to estimate the costs of a project when preparing a quotation for new work.

ZP plc has reviewed its existing client database and determined the following three average profiles of typical clients:

Client profile	D	E	F
Chargeable hours per client	100	700	300
Distance to client (miles)	50	70	100
Number of visits per client	3	8	3
Number of clients in each profile	10	5	5

Management & Cost Accounting: Professional Exam Questions.

The senior consultant has been reviewing the company's costing and pricing procedures. He suggests that the use of a single cost rate should be abandoned and, where possible, activities should be costed individually. With this in mind he has obtained the following further information:

> It is ZP plc's policy that where a visit is made to a client and the distance to the client is more than 50 miles, the consultant will travel the day before the visit and stay in local accommodation so that the maximum time is available for meeting the client the following day.

> The cost of travel to the client is dependent on the number of miles travelled to visit the client.

> Other costs are facility costs – at present the senior consultant cannot identify an alternative basis to that currently being used to attribute costs to each client.

Required:

(a) Prepare calculations to show the cost attributed to each client group using an activity-based system of attributing costs. (7 marks)

(b) Discuss the differences between the costs attributed using activity-based costing and those attributed by the current system and advise whether the senior consultant's suggestion should be adopted. (9 marks)

(c) In a manufacturing environment activity-based costing often classifies activities into: those that are: unit; batch; product sustaining; and facility sustaining. Discuss, giving examples, how similar classifications may be applied to the use of the technique in consultancy organisations such as ZP plc. (9 marks)

(25 marks)

© CIMA

24

Question 2 – May 2006, CIMA Professional Paper P2

A manager is evaluating a three-year project which has the following relevant pre-tax operating cash flow:

Year	1	2	3
	$000	$000	$000
Sales	4,200	4,900	5,300
Costs	2,850	3,100	4,150

The project requires an investment of $2 million at the start of year 1 and has no residual value.

The company pays corporation tax on its net relevant operating cash flows at the rate of 20%. Corporation tax is payable in the same year as the net relevant pre-tax operating cash flows arise. There is no tax depreciation available on the investment.

The manager has discounted the net relevant post-tax operating cash flows using the company's post-tax cost of capital of 7% and this results in a post-tax net present value of the project of $1.018 million.

Required:

(a) Briefly explain sensitivity analysis and how the manager may use it in the evaluation of this project. (4 marks)

(b) Calculate the sensitivity of the project to independent changes in

    (i) the selling price;

    (ii) the cost of capital. (6 marks)

(10 marks)

© CIMA

25

Question 7 – May 2006, CIMA Professional Paper P2

GHK manufactures four products from different combinations of the same direct materials and direct labour. An extract from the flexible budgets for next quarter for each of these products is as follows:

Product	G		H		J		K	
Units	3,000	5,000	3,000	5,000	3,000	5,000	3,000	5,000
	$000	$000	$000	$000	$000	$000	$000	$000
Revenue	30	50	60	100	45	75	90	150
Direct material A (Note 1)	9	15	12	20	4.5	7.5	18	30
Direct material B (Note 2)	6	10	6	10	13·5	22.5	36	60
Direct labour (Note 3)	6	10	24	40	22.5	37.5	9	15
Overheads (Note 4)	6	8	13	19	11	17	11	17

Notes:

1. Material A was purchased some time ago at a cost of $5 per kg. There are 5,000 kg in inventory. The costs shown in the flexible budget are based on this historical cost. The material is in regular use and currently has a replacement cost of $7 per kg.

2. Material B is purchased as required; its expected cost is $10 per kg. The costs shown in the flexible budget are based on this expected cost.

3. Direct labour costs are based on an hourly rate of $10 per hour. Employees work the number of hours necessary to meet the production requirements.

4. Overhead costs of each product include a specific fixed cost of $1,000 per quarter which would be avoided if the product is to be discontinued. Other fixed overhead costs are apportioned between the products but are not affected by the mix of products manufactured.

GHK has been advised by the only supplier of material B that the quantity of material B that will be available during the next quarter will be limited to 5,000 kg. Accordingly the company is being forced to reconsider its production plan for the next quarter. GHK has already entered into contracts to supply one of its major customers with the following:

500 units of product G
1,600 units of product H
800 units of product J
400 units of product K

Apart from this, the demand expected from other customers is estimated to be

3,600 units of product G
3,000 units of product H
3,000 units of product J
4,000 units of product K

The major customer will not accept partial delivery of the contract and if the contract with this major customer is not completed in full, then GHK will have to pay a financial penalty of $5,000.

Required:

(a) For each of the four products, calculate the relevant contribution per dollar of material B for the next quarter. (6 marks)

(b) It has been determined that the optimum production plan based on the data above is to produce 4,100 units of product G, 4,600 units of product H, 800 units of product J and 2,417 units of product K. Determine the amount of financial penalty at which GHK would be indifferent between meeting the contract or paying the penalty. (5 marks)

(c) Calculate the relevant contribution to sales ratios for each of the four products. (2 marks)

(d) Assuming that the limiting factor restrictions no longer apply, prepare a sketch of a multi-product profit volume chart by ranking the products according to your contribution to sales ratio calculations based on total market demand. Your sketch should plot the products using the highest contribution to sales ratio first.

(6 marks)

(e) Explain briefly, stating any relevant assumptions and limitations, how the multi-product profit volume chart that you prepared for question(d) may be used by the manager of GHK to understand the relationships between costs, volume and profit within the business.

(6 marks)

(25 marks)

© CIMA

26

Question 2 – November 2006, CIMA Professional Paper P2

AVN designs and assembles electronic devices to allow transmission of audio/visual communications between the original source and various other locations within the same building. Many of these devices require a wired solution but the company is currently developinga wireless alternative. The company produces a number of different devices depending on the number of input sources and the number of output locations, but the technology used within each device is identical. AVN is constantly developing new devices which improve the quality of the audio/visual communications that are received at the output locations.

The Managing Director recently attended a conference on world class manufacturing entitled "The extension of the value chain to include suppliers and customers" and seeks your help.

Required:

Explain

(i) the components of the extended value chain; and   (3 marks)

(ii) how each of the components may be applied by AVN.   (7 marks)

                                                                (10 marks)

© CIMA

27

Question 4 – November 2006, CIMA Professional Paper P2

You are the Assistant Management Accountant of QXY plc, a food manufacturer. The Board of Directors is concerned that its operational managers may not be fully aware of the importance of understanding the costs incurred by the business and the effect that this has on their operations and decision making. In addition, the operational managers need to be aware of the implications of their pricing policy when trying to increase the volume of sales.

You are scheduled to make a presentation to the operational managers tomorrow to explain to them the different costs that are incurred by the business, the results of some research that has been conducted into the implications for pricing and the importance of understanding these issues for their decision making. The diagram below has already been prepared for the presentation.

Diagram for Question Four - Costs and Revenues over a range of activity levels

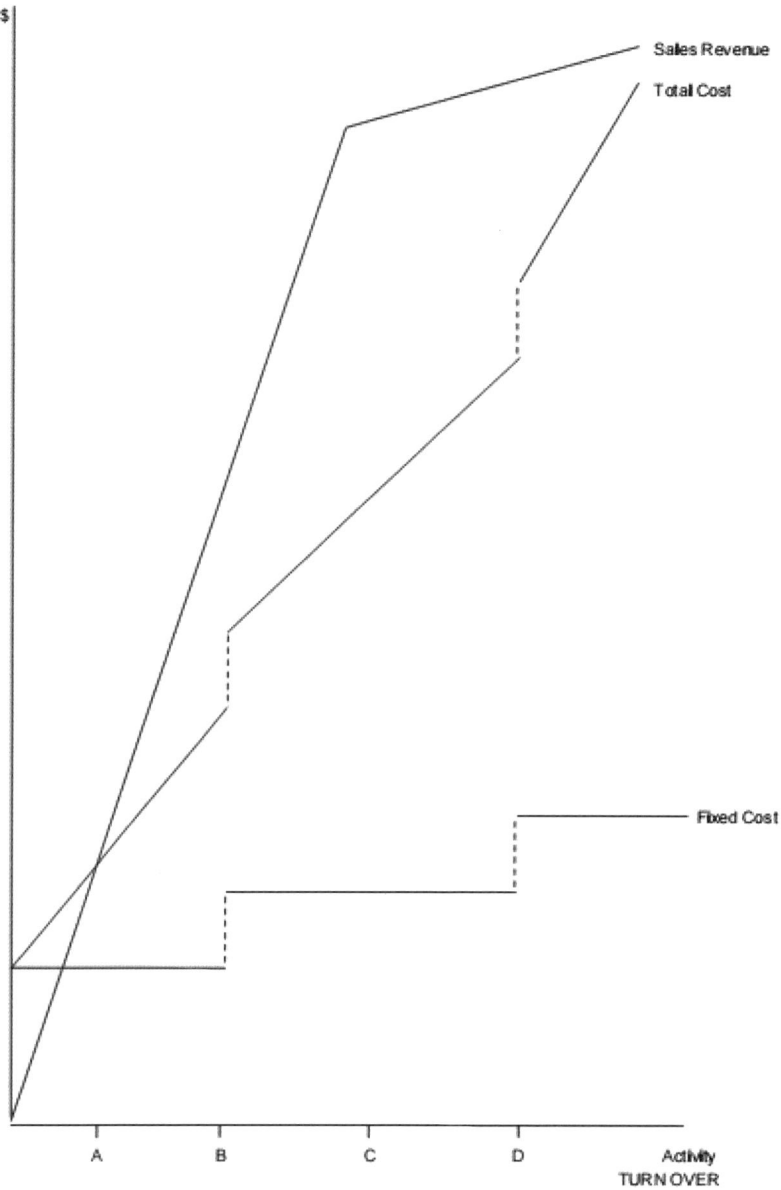

Required:

You are required to interpret the diagram and explain how it illustrates issues that the operational managers should consider when making decisions. (Note: your answer must include explanations of the Sales Revenue, Total Cost and Fixed Cost lines and the significance of each of the activity levels labelled A, B, C and D.) (10 marks)

© CIMA

28

Question 5 (c, d) – November 2006, CIMA Professional Paper P2

An analysis of the company's indirect production costs shows the following:

	$	Cost driver
Material ordering costs	220,000	Number of supplier orders
Machine set-up costs	100,000	Number of batches
Machine running costs	400,000	Number of machine hours
General facility costs	324,000	Number of machine hours

The following additional data relate to each product:

Product	W	X	Y
Machine hours per unit	5	8	7
Batch size (units)	500	400	1,000
Supplier orders per batch	4	3	5

Required:

(c) Calculate the full cost per unit of each product using Activity-Based Costing. (8 marks)

(d) Explain how Activity-Based Costing could provide information that would be relevant to the management team when it is making decisions about how to improve KL's profitability. (7 marks)

(15 marks)

© CIMA

29

Question 6 – November 2006, CIMA Professional Paper P2

A theatre has a seating capacity of 500 people and is considering engaging MS and her orchestra for a concert for one night only. The fee that would be charged by MS would be $10,000. If the theatre engages MS, then this sum is payable regardless of the size of the theatre audience.

Based on past experience of events of this type, the price of the theatre ticket would be $25 per person. The size of the audience for this event is uncertain, but based on past experience it is expected to be as follows:

People	Probability (%)
300	50
400	30
500	20

In addition to the sale of the theatre tickets, it can be expected that members of the audience will also purchase confectionery both prior to the performance and during the interval. The contribution that this would yield to the theatre is unclear, but has been estimated as follows:

Contribution from confectionery sales	Probability (%)
Contribution of $3 per person	30
Contribution of $5 per person	50
Contribution of $10 per person	20

Required:

Using expected values as the basis of your decision,

(a) advise the theatre management whether it is financially worthwhile to engage MS for the concert. (5 marks)

(b) Prepare a two-way data table to show the profit values that could occur from deciding to engage MS for the concert. (5 marks)

(c) Explain, using the probabilities provided and your answer to question (b), how the two-way data table can be used by the theatre management to evaluate the financial risks of the concert, including the probability of making a profit.

(9 marks)

(d) Calculate the maximum price that the theatre management should agree to pay for perfect information relating to the size of the audience and the level of contribution from confectionery sales. (6 marks)

(25 marks)

© CIMA

30

Question 7 – November 2006, CIMA Professional Paper P2

JK plc prepares its accounts to 31 December each year. It is considering investing in a new computer controlled production facility on 1 January 2007 at a cost of £50 million. This will enable JK plc to produce a new product which it expects to be able to sell for four years. At the end of this time it has been agreed to sell the new production facility for £1 million cash.

Sales of the product during the year ended 31 December 2007 and the next three years are expected to be as follows:

Year ended 31 December	2007	2008	2009	2010
Sales units (000)	100	105	110	108

Selling price, unit variable cost and fixed overhead costs (excluding depreciation) are expected to be as follows during the year ended 31 December 2007:

	£
Selling price per unit	1,200
Variable production cost per unit	750
Variable selling and distribution cost per unit	100
Fixed production cost for the year	4,000,000
Fixed selling and distribution cost for the year	2,000,000
Fixed administration cost for the year	1,000,000

The following rates of annual inflation are expected for each of the years during 2008–2010:

	%
Selling prices	5
Production costs	8
Selling and distribution costs	6
Administration costs	5

Management & Cost Accounting: Professional Exam Questions.
© Pearson Education Limited 2008

The company pays taxation on its profits at the rate of 30%, with half of this being payable in the year in which the profit is earned and the remainder being payable in the following year. Investments of this type qualify for tax depreciation at the rate of 25% per annum on a reducing balance basis.

The Board of Directors of JK plc has agreed to use a 12% post-tax discount rate to evaluate the investment.

Required:

(a) Advise JK plc whether the investment is financially worthwhile.   (17 marks)

(b) Calculate the Internal Rate of Return of the investment.   (3 marks)

(c) Define and contrast (i) the real rate of return and (ii) the money rate of return, and explain how they would be used when calculating the net present value of a project's cash flows.   (5 marks)

(25 marks)

© CIMA

31

Question 2 – 2005, ICAI

LIBERTINO Ltd ("LIBERTINO") is an electronic components manufacturing company. Its main product is known as "XS83" and the sales budget for the first six months of 2006 is as follows:

Month	Number of Components
January	16,000
February	18,000
March	26,000
April	24,000
May	21,000
June	20,000

The management team is now considering the raw material requirements associated with "XS83" for the first quarter of 2006. The principal raw material required for each "XS83" component is 2 kg of Material A, which costs €/£0.50/kg. In order to maintain a smooth flow of production and sales, the company has the following stock requirements:

1. The finished goods stock on hand at the end of each month will be equal to 120% of the next month's sales volume. The finished goods stock budgeted for 31 December 2005 is 19,200 components.

2. The raw material stock on hand at the end of each month will be equal to 60% of the next month's production need for materials. It is expected that there will be 22,080 kg of Material A on hand on 31 December 2005.

Note: LIBERTINO does not maintain any work-in-progress stock.

Required:

(a) (i) Prepare monthly production budgets for "XS83" for the first three months of 2006. (4 marks)

    (ii) With regard to question (i), explain briefly why the budgeted production volume varies from month to month. (3 marks)

(b) Prepare monthly budgets for the purchase of Material A (in kilograms and in euros/pounds) for the first three months of 2006. (8 marks)

Presentation Mark

(1 mark)

(c) Outline briefly TWO key criteria that a company will use when selecting a supplier to meet its raw materials needs. (4 marks)

(20 marks)

© ICAI

Management & Cost Accounting: Professional Exam Questions.
© Pearson Education Limited 2008

32

Question 2 – 2006, ICAI

FULCON Ltd. ("FULCON") is a pen manufacturing company. You have been asked to assist the company by preparing some budgets for the first three months of 2007.

The following information is available:

1. The expected sales volumes in 2007 are

January (units)	February (units)	March (units)	April (units)	May (units)	June (units)
10,000	10,500	12,000	13,000	13,500	14,000

2. The selling price per pen will be €/£3 in 2007. As in previous years, it is expected that 10% of customers will pay in the month of sale, 60% will pay in the month following sale and the remainder will pay in the month after that. The company estimates that 5% of all sales will be bad debts. Receipts of €/£32,000 and €/£15,000 respectively will arise in January and February 2007 regarding sales generated in 2006.

3. At each month end, the company typically maintains a stock (inventory) of finished goods that equals 50% of the next month's sales volume. Opening stock (inventory) of finished goods will be 5,000 units on 1 January 2007.

4. The raw materials required to manufacture the pens will cost €/£0.90 per pen. Closing stock (inventory) of raw materials valued at €/£6,000 is available on 1 January 2007 and the company requires the maintenance of this stock (inventory) level at the end of each month. The company will pay for raw materials purchases as follows:

50% in the month of purchase and

50% in the month following.

At the end of December 2006 €/£4,300 was due to creditors for purchase of raw materials.

Required:

(a) Prepare for FULCON: for each of the first THREE months of 2007 the following:

    (i) A sales revenue budget.   (2 marks)

    (ii) A schedule of the receipts from debtors.   (4 marks)

    (iii)A production budget.   (3 marks)

    (iv)A schedule of payments for purchase of raw materials.   (4 marks)

Presentation mark

(1 mark)

(b) Explain THREE ways in which you think that FULCON might accelerate its cash collection from customers.   (6 marks)

(20 marks)

© ICAI

33

Question 3 – 2006, ICAI

JANTEX Ltd ("JANTEX") manufactures all-weather jackets for use by construction workers. You have been asked to assist the company to evaluate a number of scenarios for the forthcoming year.

Fixed costs for the year are budgeted at €/£5,000,000. The budgeted selling price for each jacket will be €/£90 and the variable costs per jacket will be €/£40.

Required:

(a) Determine the breakeven point in terms of units and sales revenue.   (2 marks)

(b) Referring to the information above regarding JANTEX, draw a graph which clearly shows the following:

   (i) The revenue function.

   (ii) The total cost function.

   (iii) The breakeven point.   (6 marks)

(c) (i) Determine the profit that will be earned, if 130,000 jackets are sold in the forthcoming year.

   (ii) If 130,000 units (jackets) are sold in the forthcoming year, by what percentage can the fixed costs increase before a loss is generated?

   (iii) How many jackets must be sold to generate a profit of €/£3,000,000?

                                                                          (3 marks)

(d) The Sales Manager of JANTEX has identified that, with a small degree of modification, the jacket which the company manufactures would be suitable for use within the extreme sports industry. This modified jacket could be sold for €/£150 and would have total unit variable costs of €/£65. It is expected that producing this second jacket would increase the fixed costs of the company in the forthcoming year by €/£2,000,000. The Sales Manager recommends that sales of the modified jacket should be budgeted to make up 25% of total sales units for the forthcoming year.

Determine the breakeven point of JANTEX, in units and in euros/pounds, if both original and modified jackets are manufactured and sold in the forthcoming year. (4 marks)

(e) Describe briefly TWO assumptions of the CVP model, indicating how they may limit its usefulness in modern organisations. (4 marks)

Presentation mark

(1 mark)

(20 marks)

© ICAI

Management & Cost Accounting: Professional Exam Questions.
© Pearson Education Limited 2008

ANSWERS

1

Question 3 – June 2005, ACCA

(a) Calculation of standard profit

Budgeted machine hours = $(10,000 \times 0.3) + (13,000 \times 0.6) + (9,000 \times 0.8) = 18,000$ hours

Overhead allocation rate = $81,000/18,000 = £4.50$ per machine hour

Product	B (£)	R (£)	K (£)
Direct material	5.40	4.10	4.85
Direct labour	3.25	5.20	4.55
Fixed production overhead	1.35	2.70	3.60
Standard cost	10.00	12.00	13.00
Selling price	14.00	15.00	18.00
Standard profit	4.00	3.00	5.00

Therefore total budgeted profit is equal to £124,000.

Average standard profit per unit = $124,000/32,000 = £3.875$ per unit.

Actual sales quantity in actual mix at actual selling price *less* standard cost = £141,000.

Actual sales quantity in actual mix at standard profit = £121,000.

Actual sales quantity in standard mix at standard profit = $31,500 \times 3.875$ = £122,062.

Sales price variance = $141,000 - 121,000 = £20,000$ (F).

Sales volume profit variance = $121,000 - 124,000 = £3,000$ (A).

Sales mix profit variance = $121,000 - 122,062 = £1,062$ (A).

Sales quantity profit variance = $122,062 - 124,000 = £1,938$ (A).

Reconciliation	£	£	£
Budgeted sales at standard profit			124,000
Sales price variance		20,000 (F)	
Sales mix profit variance	1,062 (A)		
Sales quantity profit variance	<u>1,938 (A)</u>		
Sales volume profit variance		<u>3,000 (A)</u>	
			<u>17,000 (F)</u>
Actual sales at actual price less standard cost			141,000

(b) The sales mix profit variance indicates how the change in sales mix contributed to the sales volume profit variance. It shows the difference between the actual sales quantity in the actual mix and the actual sales quantity in the standard mix, valued at the standard profit per unit. The adverse variance calculated in part (a) was £1,062, indicating that the actual sales mix contained more low-margin products and fewer high-margin products. The changes in the sales mix can be shown in a tabular form as follows.

Product	Standard mix	Actual mix	Difference	Standard profit	£
B	9,844	9,500	(344)	£4	1,376 (A)
R	12,797	13,500	703	£3	2,109 (F)
K	<u>8,859</u>	<u>8,500</u>	(359)	£5	<u>1,795 (A)</u>
	31,500	31,500			1,062 (A)

The difference column indicates that more of Product R, which has the lowest standard profit, £3 per unit, was sold than was budgeted for. Less of Products B and K, which have the higher standard profits per unit, were sold than were budgeted for. Calculation of the individual mix variances for Products B, R and K does not provide information which is any more useful than that contained in the 'difference' column.

Sales mix profit variance has its significance only when products are inter-related and these relationships are taken into account at the planning stage. Only deviations from the planned sales volumes for individual products need to be investigated if products are not inter-related. In this case the products are substitutes and so are inter-related. The individual sales mix profit variances may hence be useful.

(c) A standard costing system requires preparation of standard costs, comparison of standard with actual figures, investigation of variances and instigation of corrective action if needed and review of standard costs on a regular basis.

Preparation of standard costs

Standards are required for amount of materials, labour and services required to perform a particular operation, and cost standards are derived from the standard costs of the individual operations needed to produce a given product. The quantities and costs needed for each standard can be calculated using the engineering approach or through the analysis of historical records.

The engineering approach needs a detailed study of each operation so that the materials, labour and equipment used in the operation can be verified by observation, for example by using time and motion studies.

Variance analysis

Variances derived from comparing standard costs with actual costs form the basis of cost control and support the use of responsibility accounting. A wide range of variances can be calculated, depending on the costing system employed. The causes of individual variances can be investigated in order to inform the instigation of appropriate corrective action where necessary. Both favourable and adverse variances should be investigated, as useful information can be derived from both.

Review of standard costs

Standard costs must be reviewed and updated if to retain their relevance to an organisation. The review should consider changes in the prices of inputs such as labour and materials and changes in working practices and production methods. The exception to this is the basic standard, which is left unchanged for long periods of time so that trends over time can be established. However, basic standards are not commonly used. It is more help to find ideal, current and attainable standards being used and these all need regular review.

2

Question 5 – June 2005, ACCA

(a)

TNG has a current order size of 50,000 units

Average number of orders per year = demand/order size = 255,380/50,000 = 5.11 orders

Annual ordering cost = 5.11 × 25 = £127.75

Buffer stock held = 255,380 × 28/365 = 19,591 units

Average stock held = 19,591 + (50,000/2) = 44,591 units

Annual holding cost = 44,591 × 0.1 = £4,459.10

Annual cost of current ordering policy = 4,459.10 + 127.75 = £4,587.

(b) First we have to calculate the EOQ:

EOQ = ((2 × 255,380 × 25)/0·1)^0.5 = 11,300 units

Average number of orders per year = 255,380/11,300 = 22.6 orders

Annual ordering cost = 22.6 × 25 = £565.00

Average stock held = 19,591 + (11,300/2) = 25,241 units

Annual holding cost = 25,241 × 0.1 = £2,524.10

Annual cost of EOQ ordering policy = 2,524.10 + 565.00 = £3,089

Hence, saving compared to current policy = 4,587 − 3,089 = £1,498.

(c) Annual credit purchases = 255,380 × 11 = £2,809,180

Current creditors = 2,809,180 × 60/365 = £461,783

Creditors if discount is taken = 2,809,180 × 20/365 = £153,928

Reduction in creditors = 461,783 − 153,928 = £307,855

Finance cost increase = 307,855 × 0.08 = £24,628

Discount gained = 2,809,180 × 0.01 = £28,091

Net benefit of taking discount = 28,091 − 24,628 = £3,463

The discount is financially acceptable and hence should be recommended on financial grounds.

(d) The economic order quantity (EOQ) model is based on a cost function for holding stock which has two terms: holding costs and ordering costs. Under the EOQ, the total cost of having stock is minimised when holding cost is equal to ordering cost. The EOQ model assumes certain knowledge of the variables on which it depends and therefore is called a deterministic model. Demand for stock, holding cost per unit per year and order cost are assumed to be certain and constant for the period under consideration. Actually, demand is likely to be variable or irregular and costs will not remain constant. The EOQ model also ignores the cost of running out of stock. This has caused some to suggest that the EOQ model has little to recommend it as a practical model for stock management.

The EOQ model also serves a useful purpose in directing attention towards the costs that arise from holding stock. If these costs can be decreased, working capital tied up in stock can be reduced and overall profitability can be increased. If uncertainty exists in terms of demand or lead time, a more complex stock management model using probabilities (a stochastic model) such as the Miller–Orr model can be used which calculates control limits that give guidance as to when an order should be placed.

(e) Just-in-time (JIT) stock management methods seek to minimise any waste that arises in the manufacturing process as a result of using stock. With JIT production methods, stock levels of raw materials, work-in-progress and finished goods are reduced to a minimum or eliminated altogether by improved work-flow planning and closer relationships with suppliers.

Advantages

JIT stock management methods seek to eliminate waste at all stages of the production process by minimising or eliminating stock, defects, breakdowns and production delays. This is achieved by improved work-flow planning, an emphasis on quality control and firm contracts between buyer and supplier. One advantage of JIT stock management methods is a stronger and closer relationship between buyer and supplier. This offers security to the suppliers, who benefit from regular orders, continuing future business and more certain production planning. The buyers benefit from lowered stock holding costs, lowered investment in stock and work in progress and the transfer of stock management problems to the supplier. The buyer may also benefit from purchase discounts or lower purchase costs. The emphasis on quality control in the production process reduces scrap, reworking and set-up costs, while improved production design can reduce or even eliminate unnecessary material movements. The result is a smoother flow of material and work through the production system, with no queues or idle time.

Disadvantages

A JIT stock management system may not run as smoothly in practice as theory may indicate, since there may be little room for manoeuvre in the event of unforeseen delays. The buyer is also dependent on the supplier for maintaining the quality of materials and components. If delivered quality is not up to the required level, expensive downtime or a production standstill may arise, although the buyer can protect against this eventuality by including guarantees and penalties in to the supplier's contract. If the supplier increases prices, the buyer may find that it is not easy to find an alternative supplier who is able, at short notice, to meet his standards.

3

Question 3 – June 2005, ACCA

(a) The weaknesses of traditional budgeting processes include the following:

- Many commentators, including Hope and Fraser, insist that budgets prepared under traditional processes add little value and ask for far much valuable management time which would be better spent elsewhere.

- Too heavy reliance on the 'agreed' budget has an adverse impact on management behaviour which can become dysfunctional regarding objectives of the organisation as a whole.

- The use of budgeting as a base for communicating corporate goals, setting objectives, continuous improvement, etc can be seen as contrary to the original purpose of budgeting as a financial control system.

- Most budgets are not based on a rational causal model of resource consumption but are often derived from protracted internal bargaining processes.

- Merely conformance to budget is not compatible with a drive towards continuous improvement.

(b) Benchmarking

It is arguable that because the budgetary reporting system purports to give managers 'control', there is very little real motivation to seek out benchmarks which may be used to raise budgeted performance targets. This also heavily depends upon the prevailing organisational culture, as benchmarking may be viewed as an attempt by top management to impose impossible targets upon operational managers.

Balanced scorecard

The balanced scorecard can be viewed as the addition of a few non-financial measures to the conventional budget. In an attempt to overcome this misunderstanding, many management teams now establish a performance evaluation–rewards linkage based on the achievement of scorecard targets for the forthcoming budget period. Unfortunately this can cause dysfunctional behaviour at every level within the organisation. Even in situations where the scorecard has been well designed and well implemented, it is difficult to gain widespread understanding. This is all too often because of the culture which places a very high value upon the achievement of the fixed annual targets in order to avoid the loss of status, recognition and rewards.

Activity-based models

Traditional budgets show the costs of functions and departments instead of the costs of those activities that are performed. Therefore managers have no visibility of the real 'cost drivers' of their business. In addition, it is possible that a traditional budget contains a significant amount of non-value-added costs that are not visible to the managers. The annual budget also undermines the potential of activity-based management (ABM) analysis which determines required capacity from a customer demand perspective.